LINE *Upon* LINE

GARY SHACKELFORD

ISBN 979-8-89043-614-6 (paperback)
ISBN 979-8-89043-615-3 (digital)

Christian Faith Publishing
832 Park Avenue
Meadville, PA 16335
www.christianfaithpublishing.com

Printed in the United States of America

Innocent But Proven Guilty

(Romans 5:19)

For centuries, it has been taught and accepted that mankind was born sinners, that is, sinners while in the womb. But is this what the Scriptures really teach us? After this search and examination, we will know for sure that this teaching sounds right but is not true at all.

So let us begin from Romans 5:19: "For as by one man's disobedience many were made sinners…"

Many were made sinners, not born sinners.

How then was this scripture taken out of context, and who caused this to happen? It came about from a man who was regarded as a theologian in the 3rd or 4th century (named Augustine, Bishop of

Hippo) and was added to by another theologian/a medical doctor named M.R. DeHaan, who started the radio Bible program in the 1940s. This only compounded the issue of being born in sin. (M.R. DeHaan wrote a book called "Chemistry of the Blood" which declares that sin was in the blood. His take was that the seed which was in the sperm of the man produced blood. Therefore, sin was in the blood and passed on to every living person born with sin in them in the womb. But what was really passed on to all was death, not sin, according to Romans 5:12.)

Now the scripture in Romans 9:11 says, "The children being not yet born, neither having done any good or evil." If they haven't done good or evil, they are innocent. Sin is a deed, an act of disobedience. Just as Adam & Eve were innocent until they disobeyed, so is everyone at birth.

But after being born and deposited in a society of:

1) Iniquity - which is lawlessness
2) Transgression - which is overstepping
3) Sin - which is disobedience

How could one with a fallen nature such as we have ever avoid not getting involved? (Psalm 51) This is what King David is saying in Psalm 51.

"They go astray from innocence" (Psalm 58:3). The dispensation Adam and Eve fell from was innocence; they went astray.

No one is charged with another's sin. (For where no law is, there is no transgression - Romans 4:15)

"For sin is the transgression of the law" (1 John 3:4). Had not the Lord given Adam that commandment, they could have eaten of every tree without consequence.

"Consider what I have said, and the Lord will give understanding in all things" (2 Timothy 2:7).

Why Mankind Must Repent

(Luke 13:3–5)

Repentance is not just a church ritual; it is a requirement of God throughout the pages of the whole Bible.

From the time sin was introduced into the world of men, God required sacrifice and repentance.

The sacrifice was a substitute instead of men and women dying for their sins. And except there be real sorrow for sin or godly sorrow, one will try faking his way through God's plan of salvation.

Mankind did not confess his sin nor seek forgiveness until God confronted him first, although instantly he realized he was naked, ashamed, and wrong.

Consider this: the couple could have died for their wrongdoing because they were guilty. But their lives would have been over, and without them, all humanity would be nonexistent. So to save them from eternal death and to cover their shame, the Lord God slew an animal and used that skin for a covering and blood for the sacrifice. Take note, they had already covered themselves with fig leaves, but leaves have no blood.

Now all of this was done because God wanted to save mankind from death and also deal with the sin issue. God does not tolerate sin anywhere or in anything. You must understand sin was in existence before man was on the scene. It was found in Satan and his angels, which God shall deal with them when the time comes. (Demons said, "Are you come to destroy us before the time?" [Matthew 8:29, Luke 4:34])

Now in the case of mankind, sin caused death. In order to eradicate death, sin must be eradicated, and the one who caused sin must be eradicated.

All in due time, but until we are all saved and taken out of this situation, repentance and water baptism in the name of Jesus Christ is absolutely the only way to be saved (Acts 4:12). None other name given under heaven whereby we (all) must be saved.

Now if repentance does not come with a broken heart or spirit, it is fruitless. Now mind you, I am not talking about tears and sorrow, because tears and sorrow are not true repentance. A thief can be sorry, but sorry because they got caught, not sorry for the deed.

The scriptures say Judas repented, and he was also sorry. But he went and hung himself. That's sorrow and sadness but not brokenness. True repentance leads one to God, not leads one away from God. All need to understand that without Christ becoming the sacrifice, mankind would face eternal damnation as long as God lives. There is no such thing as purgatory. If one does not get themselves together in this life, forget about a life on the other side. Because after this life, there is the judgement, which no man shall escape (Revelation 20:11–15).

Let me explain; when we were naturally born, our names were written in a register, and a certificate was issued signifying that we were born alive (one can be born dead/without a spirit).

So in the spirit, one must be born again, and their names would be written in the Lamb's book of life. When one dies naturally, another certificate is issued stating that you are dead. If in the time of one's life one does not get saved by repentance and water baptism into Jesus Christ, all is lost for all eternity.

> It is not the will of God
> that any should perish, but that
> all should come to repentance.
> (2 Peter 3:9)

The last word on this is most people think that when this life is over, it's over. But look at it this way: when something perishes, it is not annihilated; it's still here but changed for another purpose. When writing paper is burned, its purpose for clear writing is changed. But now the carbon that is left can be used for something else. So in effect, it's never going to be over. Just changed.

Men must repent! That's not a "guess so"; that's an "even so."

Composed and written by overseer
Gary Shackelford

Was God Ever Born?

(Originally written July 16, 2021)

*For unto you is born this day in the city
of David a Savior, which is Christ the Lord.*

—Luke 2:11

It has been taught down through the years that Jesus is God, which is correct. And that He was God and man at the same time. But that raises two specific questions?

    (1) Was He born God?
    (2) And if so, does that make Mary the mother of God?

Reasoning would make this so. However, the Scriptures teach us that God always was and always will be. He never had a beginning and will never have an end. He is eternal. So let's examine the mystery of the Godhead. Did God become the man Christ Jesus in the flesh? Or did the man Christ Jesus become flesh made spirit? That is God.

Let us keep this scripture in mind throughout this writing: "I am the Lord, I change not" (Malachi 3:6).

If God cannot change, He could not then become flesh, especially ("vile" flesh). But flesh could be changed. So God birthed a whole human man (body, soul, spirit) and called that man Jesus Christ. The spirit of God entered into Him in the form of the Holy Ghost at His baptism and began to reconcile the world to Himself (Hebrews 2:14–16, 2 Corinthians 5:19). At death, the spirit left that body dead on Calvary. Got back into that body at the resurrection (but not without changing flesh to spirit/Christ rose in a glorified spiritual body), living a natural life in the flesh first; resurrecting to a life in the spirit, second. As the Scriptures have said: "First that which is natural, then that which is spiritual" (1 Corinthians 15:46).

He had to go back on high for two reasons:

(1) Because He was now God in the flesh/ returned to where He was before
(2) To mediate for mankind in heaven in the high priest office

The spirit changed not itself, but it changed the natural flesh body into a spiritual body that could live forever. So the flesh died but not the spirit.

If God, being a spirit, was birthed from Mary's womb, then Mary would not only be God's mother, but it would be that God died on Calvary, and that God rose from the dead. The *Word* from the beginning was the thought of God. It was the thought that became flesh, not the spirit.

Now because the Word was with God from the beginning, and God has no beginning, no thought of God could ever have a beginning without God. So the Word became a living man and was later exalted after death to become a life-giving spirit in the form of human flesh.

> Behold my hands and my
> feet; that it is I myself; handle
> me and see; for a spirit hath not

flesh and bone as ye see me have.
(Luke 24:39)

The only life-giving spirit is God. Now this Word or man was made Lord and Christ (Acts 2:37). God as a spirit was never made anything. In the human flesh, Jesus was called the Son of Man/human first. In the spirit, Jesus is called the Son of God (Romans 1:4), declared or revealed (seen) by the resurrection from the dead.

Take notice, no angel worshiped Him at His birth (Luke 2) because the Word was human. But when the glorified spirit-God-man returns to the world "let all the angels of God worship Him" (Hebrews 1).

How did this mix-up begin? A man in the third or fourth century came up with a saying called the *hypostatic union*, which is God and man at the same time. He placed that union at the birth of this man from Mary instead of at the resurrection of this man, whereby proclaiming Him God while in the womb.

Many don't know what the immaculate conception is really all about. It is not about Jesus being born of a virgin. It's about Mary being born a virgin; from a virgin, meaning her mother, Elizabeth, was declared a virgin also.

This notion or concept was not accepted when it first came about, but because this man had great influence on many others, it slowly took hold over the centuries on what is called Christendom. You will find no such allusion by the apostles or scriptures of this concept. This man was a church father but not of the Christian faith. He was of Roman Catholicism which incorporates heathen traditions into a form of worship and teaches this for doctrine. Jesus at His resurrection was declared or revealed as God in the flesh, whereby He could appear and disappear, walk through doors, or remain invisible. He, Jesus, was made both Lord (that is God) and Christ (that is Savior) at His resurrection.

> Thou art my Son; this day
> have I begotten thee. (Psalms 2:7,
> Hebrews 1:)

Jesus became a begotten Son twice:

1)   At His natural birth (only begotten Son)
2)   A begotten Son from the death (first begotten Son from the dead)

Why Men Sin

(Romans 7:18–23)

Romans 6 speaks of two bodies: "Every living person has this in them." Having this "nature" in all, all will sin.

First John 1:7–10 lets us know none can say, "We have no sin." Reinforcing this, Galatians 3:19–22 informs us, "All are concluded under sin"

1)   "The body of sin must be destroyed."

One must become partakers of the "divine nature" through water baptism [in Jesus's name] and the divine nature (2 Peter 1:4): "gift of the Holy Ghost."

Principle of sin or sin "nature":

2)   "Let not sin reign in your mortal body."

Carnal or physical body.
The two are inseparable until death.
Death is because of sin, yet death at the same time frees one from sin. But if one dies in sin, they are held in death forever.
Death will not disappear until sin disappears "because the last enemy that shall be destroyed is death" (1 Corinthians 15:26).

> It's no more I that do it, but
> 'sin that dwelleth in me. (Romans
> 7:17–20)

> By nature the children of
> wrath. (Ephesians 2:1–3)

Sin is not an ingredient; it's a characteristic. Disobedience is found in the nature of man. Only God can and has tackled the issue of sin. No angel or other power could.

Is Sin an Ingredient or a Characteristic?

It has been taught for centuries that sin is in the blood. And it was the sole reason why Jesus was conceived by the Holy Ghost because the seed of man (semen/blood) was contaminated with sin.

All of this is because a radio preacher, who was also a medical doctor, taught that sin was in the blood, and it was widely accepted. They even try to justify his teaching by scripture saying "I was shaped in iniquity" (Psalms 51) and "conceived in sin"—in other words, I was in sin in my mother's womb; therefore, I came out a sinner.

The meaning of Psalms 51 by the so-called "early church fathers" (Catholic church fathers) was misinterpreted.

There are three key words in Psalms 51 that point us in the right direction if we follow it correctly.

1. Iniquity
2. Transgression
3. Sin

Iniquity means "lawlessness."
Transgression means "overstepping."
Sin means "disobedience."

But is this what the Scriptures teach us? Let's take a close look at what the Scriptures really teach us. Lawlessness cannot be without "a law or rule." Transgression cannot be without "a law or rule." Sin cannot be without "a law or rule."

Three different words apply to one thing: "a law or rule."

> By the law is the knowledge
> of sin. (Romans 3:20)

> For where no law is, there is
> no transgression. (Romans 4:15)

> Sin is not imputed when
> there is no law. (Romans 5:13)

So we see that sin is not an ingredient; it is a characteristic. In other words, in "our nature."

Adam's nature changed when he sinned. His nature became *fallen*. This was the fallen nature that was passed on to Adam's children. We are all born with a fallen nature. As Adam started out in innocence, so we start out in innocence: "We go astray as soon as we be born, speaking lies" ((Psalms 58:3) because by nature we are children of wrath (Ephesians 2:3).

This is the reason the Holy Ghost is given to us because it is the holy or divine nature of God.

The nature of God is a holy nature, much unlike our unholy nature. Every living person is born with human nature. That is the character of man. But the character of man is corrupt. This again is why every man must be born again because it is the only way by birth does one get a nature. No other way can one get the nature of God without being born of God.

The Human Soul Is
Not Immortal

It has been taught for decades that the soul of man is immortal, and at death only the body is dissolved. This, again, is a teaching of great misunderstanding. Where did this teaching come from? Of course, it mostly came from Greek influence (classical period of Greece).

The Bible gives us a very clear picture of what a soul is. In the book of Genesis, God made man of the dust of the earth, and breathed into him spirit, and man became a living soul. Lying there on the ground before receiving breath, man was still a soul, a dormant one, but still a soul.

The whole man is made up of a three-part composition called a soul. There is a visible part (body) and two invisible parts (mental and spiritual), a tripartite so to speak. Impossible to be separated. While living, he is a soul; and in death, he is still a soul. The soul was made from dust. The body is the outer or visible part of the soul. If you have killed the body, you have killed the soul; if you killed the soul, you have killed the body.

Two passages of scripture speak of souls in this way: "Eight souls were saved" (1 Peter 3:20) and "Souls of them slain" (Revelation 6:9). It is clear that the scriptures were not speaking of something invisible or not tangible. It's speaking of bodies. Man was made with a body and will continue with a body throughout eternity (2 Corinthians 5).

Now having established what a soul is, let us see if this same soul is immortal. The Greeks thought that because the soul was invisible, it was eternal. But consider these scriptures: God "only has immortality dwelling in the light which no man can approach unto: no man has seen nor can see" (1 Timothy 6:15–16) and God "brought life and immortality to light through the gospel" (2 Timothy 1:10).

> We that seek for glory and
> honor and immortality. (Romans
> 2:7)

This mortal shall have put
on immortality. (1 Corinthians
15:53–54)

This tabernacle [body] mor-
tality [would be swallowed up] by
life [immortality]. (2 Corinthians
5:1–4)

How can we put on what we already would have
had if we had never lost it? From the beginning, man
never had immortality or eternal life. That would
have come after his life of obedience.

That's why the soul that sinneth (that is the person) shall die.

You cannot kill that which is eternal; neither
can sickness or any other thing destroy or interfere
with its life.

The Difference Between Light and Darkness

(August 18, 2022)

According to the scriptures, the difference between light and darkness is more important than just the separation of day from night. It has to do with where one will spend eternity.

In the Genesis 1 account, two things were going on at the same time. There was a natural darkness and a spiritual darkness. Many don't understand that when life is spiritually messed up, so is the natural life. When Adam fell into sin spiritually, his whole natural life changed, even to the point that his human nature was now changed and corrupt (Ephesians 2:1–3). We are born by nature the enemy of God because the DNA of Adam was passed on to us. Therefore, the DNA (divine nature) of the Spirit of God is passed on to us by birth *being born again* (2 Peter 1:4).

As we were born of Adam in darkness, so are we born of God in light (inheritance of the saints in light) (Colossians 1:12).

According to the scriptures, Adam died the same day that he sinned, although he lived a natural life until he was 930 years old. He would not have died at all had he followed the instructions given. In the natural world, darkness is a result of the absence of natural light. So in the spiritual world, death is the result of the absence of spiritual life, which life is God Himself (in Him was life; and the life was the light of men [John 1:4; Luke 22:47–43] power of darkness; delivered us from the power darkness [Colossians 1:9–13]; "they fell backward" [John 18:1–14]).

So let's look at this scripture in John 1:4: "In him was life; and the life was the light of men." Would it make a difference if the scripture said, "In him was light; and the light was the life of men"? It is really the same thing being said: His life is the light of men because men are in darkness.

Now, that darkness is a result of the works of the devil in our minds and fallen human nature (enemies in our minds by wicked works [Colossians 1:13–21]). When the devil and his angels sinned, they left their habitation (leaving the holiness of truth and light of God). They chose death with its darkness, and therefore God bound them in chains (confined them in darkness, *skotos*); the darkness became their chains (Jude 6; 2 Peter 2:4) to reserve them until their judgment.

Now, in the case of men, the darkness of sin is their prison. When the scriptures speak of the spirits in prison, it is not talking about the fallen angels; it's talking about the spirits of mankind being in their own prison of sin in Noah's day (1 Peter 3:18–20)—that is the only time scripture makes mention of spirits being in prison in the time of Noah.

In the book of Isaiah (61:1), it speaks about Jesus opening the prison and releasing the captives, yet we did not see one time when Jesus went to any prison; not even when His cousin John was in prison did Jesus ever go to a prison. So what were the scriptures referring to when it said "opening of the prisons"? That has to do with being bound by sin in darkness.

In the book of John 3:17–21, Jesus speaks of light and darkness (*skotos*): "Men love darkness because their deeds [works] were evil."

The light that Jesus speaks of is the light of the glory of God. To put it plainly, God is that light. People think that when God says that through Jesus Christ life is given, life is not separate from God; life is God. This is why when anyone dies, the spirit of life goes back to where it came from but not in a conscious state (Ecclesiastes 12:7).

Since God is life and spirit, life goes back to life. Since the fall of man, the world of man was plunged in the darkness of the devil (which is sin). But let's look at sin in this light; all sin is disobedience, and that disobedience is toward God. Its penalty and consequence are death.

Death is like cold. The absence of heat makes cold. The absence of life is death. Since then God is life and eternal, death is the absence of life eternally.

Since God is light, the opposite or absence of light is darkness.

Were We Born in Sin, and Is Sin Really in the Blood?

"Born in sin" and "sin in the blood" are not found at all in the scriptures. They are the product of a man-made assumption and misunderstanding of scriptures (teaching for doctrine, the commandments of men [Matthew 15:9]). I know we have been taught these things for decades, but that alone does not make them true.

Now I say "commandments of men" because it was three centuries later that "born in sin" was fabricated by a man named St. Augustine, who said that sin was transmitted by sexual intercourse. He did not say how this could come about but that it traveled from generation to generation by sexual intercourse and conception. He called it original sin. The Bible does not speak of original sin, yet if there is an original sin, it would be the sin of unbelief.

The scriptures do not agree with this concept. No sin is passed on because of someone else's wrongdoing. What was passed on to us from Adam was the nature of sin. Sin is a deed, a work that is not transferable (every man according as his work shall be).

Since we all have the nature of sin, it is impossible for us not to sin. Sin cannot be without a law or rule being broken (sin is not imputed/chargeable where there is no law [Romans 5:13]). A gun by itself is not breaking any law except when it is owned illegally. Loading that gun is not illegal. Firing that gun is not illegal. Using that same gun illegally is wrong, even if that gun was not loaded. So what was passed on to us from Adam was not sin itself but the nature of sin. From the nature of sin comes forth sin, and death from sin; so all are concluded under sin, so death passes upon all men (Romans 5:12–14).

For as by one man's sin many were made sinners (not born sinners [Romans 5:19]). So all are born innocent until they sin. Adam was created innocent until he sinned, not before. God knew Adam was going to sin before God made him. But God did not charge Adam with sin until he sinned. Adam was innocent.

Now from this concept, a man by the name of Mr. De Haan, a medical doctor and founder of the radio Bible program and a preacher in 1943, published a book called *Chemistry of the Blood*. In this book, De Haan declares that the reason Joseph, Mary's husband, was not to be Jesus's father was that sin was in his blood, or he had sinful blood. And that through blood, sin is transmitted. He contends that the blood (from father's sperm) in the child while the mother makes only the body. Otherwise, Jesus would be a sinner.

This concept was accepted by almost all that is called Christendom to this day. Some believe that the seed comes from the male, which is what De Haan believed, and the seed is the sperm of the male. *Seed* concerning men in the scriptures means offspring. If *seed* means sperm, would the seed of the woman mean "the sperm of the woman" and would produce the child? Women don't have sperm.

Now, because De Haan was a doctor and preacher and well-accepted, there were not many who challenged this theory. And because it made sense to them, it was accepted as biblical true doctrine. No scripture speaks of sin in the blood, or sinful blood, or sinless blood, or holy blood. Sin is not in the blood; it's in the nature.

About the Author

Overseer Gary Shackelford is the founder and pastor of the Shekinah Glory Apostolic Church, Inc. Pastor Shackelford and Lady Rosalind were both saved in June 1967 at the Lily of the Valley Bible Way Church in Philadelphia, Pennsylvania. His ministry began as a teaching deacon two years later at the same church. Through the years, he was elevated from deacon to minister, to evangelist, and finally, to elder. He remained for twenty-two years until the former pastor, Sadie Gravely, transitioned. Pastor Shackelford became the pastor there under the organizational name Gravely Memorial Faith Bible Way Church in November 1989. For ten years, he pastored there until his vision for the Shekinah Glory Apostolic Church, Inc. work began in February 1999. Pastor Shackelford was again elevated to the overseer position in the organization called World Assembly of Restoration (WAR), which his church group joined in 1999. Pastor Shackelford resides in the state of Delaware with his wife, Evangelist Rosalind, of fifty-nine years (faithful in ministry and first lady of Shekinah Glory Apostolic Church, Inc.).